THE GARDEN

OF

INFINITE POSSIBILITIES

ALEX ACQUARONE

Illustrated by Sophia Kountzeri

Title: "The Garden of Infinite Possibilities"

Author: Alex Acquarone

Cover and Illustrations: Sophia Kountzeri

Original Title: "Il Giardino delle Infinite Possibilità"

English Translation: Marina Petruzzi

Editing: Sophia Kountzeri

First Edition: July 2015

ISBN 979-1220003292

www.thegardenofinfinitepossibilities.com

Magic

is what happens

when mind

forgets about its limits.

Contents

INTRODUCTION

This is a simple story, suitable for children of all ages: young and... old!

Every individual has his own identity, culture and beliefs.

Before reading this story, it is best to put all that aside.

Ideally, it is best to strip of all preconceptions and beliefs regarding reality and dress the part of a child, just like the main character of the story.

This book is filled with questions.

The answers are just *my* answers; they do not claim to be *the* truth and are provided with full respect to differing opinions.

My intent is not to give solutions, but to encourage free thinking.

I will have achieved my goal if even just one child in the world, after reading this book, will begin to ask himself questions and begin looking for answers: *his own* answers.

I will also be enormously happy if that same child, during his musings, shall discover that he is *already* perfect and infinite, as infinite are the possibilities of achieving his dreams, just here and now.

With all my heart, I hope that child… will be YOU!

"When I meet a child,
I feel two different emotions:
tenderness, for what he is,
respect, for what he can become."
(Louis Pasteur)

To myself,

to my children,

and to all the children of the world.

THE DREAMER

CHAPTER ONE

"Jimi! Stop day-dreaming!" said the teacher. "Jimi! JIMIII!"

"Huh? Oh… yes Miss … I was trying to figure out how to solve the math problem on the board …" said Jimi, distracted as usual.

"Don't make matters worse by lying!" the teacher went on.

"I definitely have to speak to your mother and tell her how you've been behaving in class: just good for nothing!"

BRRRING! Rang the bell and all the students dashed out the door, eager to get to their little lunches and enjoy a carefree afternoon.

The teacher left as well, slamming the door behind her, all uptight and completely full of herself.

Jimi remained seated for a couple of minutes, staring into space, trying to remember the only thing that mattered to him: *his dream.*

Shortly there after, he was out on the street and inside a flashy, noisy, smoke filled box which human beings call "cities". The traffic was intense and everyone seemed crazed, racing at top speed to who knows where, honking their horns and not even acknowledging one another.

The few parks available were filled with children joyfully playing. The street leading towards home was lined with shops that overflowed with enticing objects and foods.

But he wasn't the least bit interested in any of this.

Ever since he was little, Jimi was attracted to the ***invisible***.

As he walked alone, swinging his backpack around, he

pondered many questions: Why am I here? Who am I? How does life work? How do I accomplish my dreams? And most important: Why won't anyone answer my questions?

Once again, not having received any answers to his questions that day; he arrived at his garden, one of the few places that truly interested him.

He didn't know why, but he found it to be a magical place. Everything there just flowed smoothly: there was no scolding, and every month different colored flowers bloomed. To enjoy this wonder, he didn't have to spend his pennies; he could stay there even if he didn't do well in his class work. He didn't have to talk or make jokes to get others to like him. No one asked anything of him.

It was the perfect place to just lie down and gaze at the sky with its ever-changing clouds.

"Jimi! Did you do your homework? Did you tidy up your room? Come and help me with the laundry!" his mom yelled.

"The fun's over!" he thought to himself, reluctantly walking towards other things he "had" to do, giving up his special moments of peace.

His mom talked all the time. She gave orders and told him all the things that had gone wrong that day, just to get them off her chest: the problems at work, things she blamed others for, the bills that needed to be paid and the huge efforts she made to provide for her family ever since her husband had left.

Jimi quietly listened to her, or rather "heard" her without really listening, commenting every now and again with an: "Eh, yes."; "Of course!"; "I understand Mom." just to make her happy; otherwise it would be as though she was speaking to a wall!

The only person in the family that really fascinated him was Lili, his little sister. She was always happy and looked at everything with curiosity. She seemed to live in another dimension. She could spend an entire afternoon tirelessly playing with the same object, even if others found it to be insignificant.

Jimi loved her and protected her.

Lili brought him back to a time when he was just as carefree and unburdened by all those unanswered questions in his head.

Then there was Mark, his mom's boyfriend. He would get home late in the afternoon and while waiting for dinner, would plant himself in front of the TV and rant about the daily news.

Jimi lived in an ordinary family, in an ordinary city, in an ordinary time, but he was not just an ordinary boy.

He was a *genius*. Only, he didn't know it yet.

That evening was like any other: the usual dinner awaited him.

But something began to shift, in the most peculiar way…

The Night of a Thousand Colors

Chapter Two

Jimi was helping set the table, when suddenly, his mother's voice thundered from the kitchen:

"Jimi! Come here right now! Look, this is an email from your teacher: she says you don't pay attention in class, that you're distracted and that… you lie!"

"But… mom… I can explain …"

"I don't want to hear any excuses!" she said. "Tonight you're grounded: no TV and you're going to bed right after dinner!"

Jimi was mortified.

He couldn't help it that he had so many dreams swimming around in his head, while he was at school!

He felt good for nothing, just like his teacher had said.

Moments later, still upset by his mother's yelling, Jimi slipped on one of Lili's toys, spilling the soup all over the floor. No sooner did his mother have a chance to scold him, when Mark – hungry and ready to have dinner – got up from the couch and started ranting at Jimi, telling him, that he was "good for nothing!"

Feeling worse by the minute, he struggled to fight back tears that threatened to burst, and began to clean up the mess on the floor. He thought himself to be truly worthless and that maybe, life was just becoming too difficult for him.

Then, his mother prepared something else for dinner: a nice pasta dish for everyone.

The atmosphere at the table was tense, in part due to Jimi's conduct, in part due to the financial issues that the family was facing, and in part due to the fact that Jimi's mother and Mark weren't exactly happy together.

On that grey evening, the only happy one was Lili who paid no attention to any of the "adult" problems, as she played with a cork, sending it spinning every which way.

But the worse had yet to come.

By the end of dinner, Mark asked Jimi: "Where did you put the baseball bat I lent you yesterday? The one I played with in high school, my pride and joy…"

Jimi thought back. He felt a cold shiver run down his spine. It seemed as though time had stopped. For a few long moments he didn't know whether to lie or tell the truth. He chose the latter and confessed that he had forgotten it on the playing field - which was basically like saying he had lost it.

They were too upset to even yell at Jimi.

His mother, disappointed, said nothing and began to clear the table. Mark, with an icy, angry tone, placed a hand on Jimi's shoulder and said: "You're good for nothing, boy!" and went to lie down on the couch.

It's hard to describe how Jimi felt that evening, as he climbed up the stairs that led to his room.

As soon as he entered his "refuge", he put on some random pajamas, climbed into bed, and once under the covers burst out crying, burying his head in the pillow so that no one would hear him.

His head was bursting with sorrow, but most of all with anger, toward a world that *he* didn't understand and that didn't understand *him*.

In that moment, he really missed his father, who was an introverted yet happy man; a dreamer who spoke little and taught by example. The loving adult figure, he now wanted most by his side.

Jimi was sad, disheartened and lonely, feeling evermore "good for nothing".

That night, before falling asleep, he did something unusual: he looked out into the starry sky and asked if there was a God, an angel, or anyone who truly cared about him and who could answer his questions.

Sobbing, he began saying: "Dear God, I don't know if you exist and I don't know what your name is. However, if you're listening, please know that I'm desperate and I need help. I ask you with all of my heart, the heart of a child: please answer my questions! Who am I? What am I doing here? Why doesn't anyone understand me? How can I be happy?"

He received no answer. He saw no God.

The sky remained blue. The moon remained full. The stars remained still and brilliant.

Jimi felt a great sense of peace, after having poured his heart out, as though an invisible caress had lightly touched and soothed him. Soon he was sound asleep, exhausted after such a difficult day.

That night his sleep was filled with dreams. Brilliant colors flowed one after the other: pink, gold, blue, azure, green, yellow, violet, orange, and many others, whose names he didn't even know. He heard soft music, saw thousands of birds flying in an endless sky.

A wave of sweetness washed over his soul.

At a certain point in time, he slowly opened his eyes, still in bliss from the marvel of his dream, he saw the colors slowly fading one after the other, like a sunset. But, in the darkness of his room only one color had remained: blue! It was an intense blue, deep yet very luminous: like a sapphire with the moonlight reflecting off of it.

Jimi rubbed his eyes as, at the foot of his bed on the couch, he saw a spot of that luminous blue which seemed to be alive.

Looking closer… it was alive!

It was the outline of a person!

Normally, Jimi would have been scared out of his wits, but that dream with the thousand colors had infused so much peace in him, that he managed to remain still enough to get a better look.

Sitting on the couch was a man in his thirties, very peaceful and relaxed, wrapped in a cape the color of a most radiant blue; so radiant in fact that it seemed as though it wasn't even fabric: it was pure energy!

"Who are you?" asked Jimi shyly.

"I am a master teacher." answered the man with a steady yet sweet voice, giving the boy just a glimpse of his face from under the hood.

"Oh no! Not another teacher! I already have plenty of those to deal with at school…"

"I don't teach any subjects, I don't judge, I don't give grades. I'm a master of life. *My* life." answered the man.

"What are you doing in my room?" said Jimi.

"I'm here because you asked for help. Last night I heard your prayers, the same prayers that were once my very own. Just like you, when I was a child I went through some difficult times and I was full of questions. Then, I found the answers and turned my life into the masterpiece it deserved to become."

"So… no class work? No tests?" asked Jimi.

"No, my dear boy. Just a friendly chat between the two of us, if you like."

"Yeah, great! But… should I call you 'master'?" asked Jimi.

"You can call me whatever you want!" the man answered, amused.

"I'll call you Blu, like the color of your beautiful cape!" said Jimi, curious and vibrant like he hadn't been in a long time.

"Perfect! What would you like to know? What's your first question?" asked Blu.

"My first question is…" began Jimi.

"Wait! – Blu interrupted him – Do not just believe my answers!"

"Why not?"

"Because, what I'm going to tell you is not *the* truth: it's ***my*** truth." Blu explained. "So I ask, that you to verify my words, through your own reasoning and through practical experience. Only when you have turned into experience, all that I have told you, will it become *your* truth as well. Otherwise, it will all just remain a fairy tale. Understood?"

"Ok, deal! – said Jimi – Now, my first question is: why did I have such a bad day today?"

"Because you created it with your thoughts!" answered Blu.

"ME?!? But it's not my fault! Today I had nothing but bad luck!" said the boy.

"Think about it, Jimi. Ever since the teacher scolded you this morning, what thought has been constantly going through your mind? What do you think of yourself?"

"Umm… that I'm good for nothing." said Jimi.

"And what kind of day did you create for yourself, with that thought in mind?"

"A day filled with disasters. A day... good for nothing!" answered the child sadly.

"There! You see? You figured it out by yourself." said Blu.

"So, my small, insignificant thoughts that no one knows about can make things happen? Please Blu, explain to me how this is possible!"

"I'd be happy to! – Blu answered – But you'll have to come with me… to the *Garden of Infinite Possibilities*!"

The Garden of Infinite Possibilities

Chapter Three

All of a sudden, Jimi's room was transformed into a most wondrous landscape: a crystal clear blue sky lay over a vibrant green meadow, which stretched all the way to the horizon and in every direction.

"Here we are! – said Blu – Welcome… to the Garden of Infinite Possibilities!"

"Wow! It's great!" exclaimed Jimi amazed.

"Here there are only three rules." Blu explained.

"Rule number 1: *There are infinite possibilities.*"

"Rule number 2: *Thoughts become things.*"

"And Rule number 3?" asked Jimi.

"*Never forget the first two rules*!" answered Blu.

The boy was astonished.

"Now let's have some fun, Jimi! – Blu said – Think of something you want to grow in this garden."

"Let's see… – thought Jimi – I'd like … a cherry tree! You know, I love cherries. They remind me of summertime feasts. They give me a sense of **abundance**!"

No sooner had Jimi finished his sentence, when a majestic cherry tree appeared before him.

"Wow! – Jimi exclaimed – Now, I'd like … some red roses! They remind me of when my dad used to bring my mom roses, as a sign of his **love**."

Then, the most beautiful roses in the world appeared in the garden.

"Can I wish for animals too?" asked Jimi.

"Rule number 1 – Blu reminded him – *There are infinite possibilities*!"

"Then… I'd like a dog. Dogs remind me of **playing**! Also, lots and lots of birds! They remind me of **freedom**! As well as some daisies, lilies, sunflowers and tulips, so we have some **variety**."

Like magic, that enormous green meadow was filled with thousands of flowers, plants and animals, all according to Jimi's thoughts.

"But how did it happen? Is it magic?"

"The scientific reason as to how this happened, you'll learn tomorrow in school." answered Blu.

"Tomorrow? How do you know?"

"Let's stay focused on the Garden of Infinite Possibilities. –said Blu – You've created a wonderful reality, congratulations!"

"Thanks!" said Jimi, satisfied.

"As I'm sure you realize, thanks to your thoughts, you have created in the garden of your life: **ABUNDANCE** (the cherry trees); **LOVE** (the roses); **PLAY** (the dog); **FREEDOM** (the birds) and

VARIETY (the flowers). How beautiful!"

"It's true! These are all emotions that make me feel good!" The boy happily smiled.

"Excellent, Jimi! Now that you've created this wonderful garden – Blu continued – do you think it makes sense to create, for example: spiders, snakes, flies, mosquitoes, mud, swamps, and storms?"

Jimi thought about this scenario and just moments later, the flower-filled garden became a horrible swamp, the weather turned dark, as spiders, snakes and insects of all kinds began to pop up everywhere.

"No, no! This is horrible! Please, turn it back to the way it was!" Jimi begged, upset.

Blu observed the garden and in seconds, once again, everything had become radiant.

"Rule number 2: *Thoughts become things.*" said Blu. "**ALL** thoughts become things. It doesn't matter if they're good thoughts or bad thoughts: the garden does not judge, it simply creates what you think."

He went on to explain: "What often happens to people, is that they either don't know this rule or they just forget it. So, apart from a few pleasant thoughts, they start allowing unpleasant thoughts into their lives, like **SADNESS, ANGER, VIOLENCE, POVERTY, DIFFICULTY, DOUBT** or **UNWORTHINESS**. Just as I attempted to show you before, with all those unwelcome guests in your beautiful garden."

"But it doesn't make sense! – exclaimed the boy – Who in their right mind would do something like that?"

"Think about it, Jimi… What did you think about yourself all day yesterday and what did you create with those thoughts?"

"Umm… that I was good for nothing. And… well… yeah! I created a disastrous day." answered Jimi disheartened.

"Do you think that's very different from inviting snakes, insects, swamps and storms into the garden of your life?" asked Blu.

"No. I guess not … – answered Jimi – I polluted my very own garden!"

"Well yes! – Blu smiled – Our job is to create the garden of our dreams and to monitor our thoughts so that unpleasant things don't grow there."

"Ok! I'll remember that!" the boy said.

"I'm proud of you, Jimi! Tonight you have learned some very important concepts! Would you like to tell me what they are?"

"There are three rules. – Jimi quickly answered – Rule n. 1: *There are infinite possibilities.* Rule number 2: *Thoughts become things.* Rule number 3: *Never forget the first two rules*!"

"Excellent! – Blu exclaimed – Now you better get some sleep. You have school tomorrow."

"Ok." agreed Jimi… even though he was completely electrified and had absolutely no desire to go back to sleep!

"By the way … – Blu provoked him – What kind of day would you like to create tomorrow? How do you want to think of yourself, Jimi?"

"Well, if at first I thought of myself as good for nothing – answered the boy – now I'm going to think that… I have always been a GENIUS!"

"Wonderful! Sweet dreams!" said Blu.

Needless to say, Jimi didn't get much sleep: he spent the rest of the night staring into space, his eyes wide open, fantasizing about his infinite possibilities!

A Sea of Waves

Chapter Four

COCKADOODLEDOOOOO!!! Jimi's alarm clock rang at 7:00 AM sharp.

Still jazzed after that bizarre night, he got up happy and full of energy. He got dressed quicker than usual, inhaled his breakfast without complaining and dashed out the door to catch the school bus, all the while repeating to himself: "*I have always been a genius!*"

As soon as he got to school, he saw an unusual scene: a group of children were pushing and hitting the vending machine trying to get it to work.

All this fuss was happening, due to the fact that Susie, the prettiest girl in the class – who never acknowledged Jimi – had put her money in the machine but… the snack wouldn't come out!

Jimi thought: "I'm a genius, so I'll find the solution!"

As everyone continued to use physical force to get the snack to fall, Jimi calmly observed from afar, and noticed that the machine was slightly tilted because of a small wooden wedge that had been inserted underneath during maintenance.

With the help of one of his friends, he removed the wedge and just like magic, Susie's snack came out.

She gave him the sweetest look and said: "Thanks Jimi, you're a genius!"

He was in seventh heaven, first of all because he really liked Susie, and secondly, because his thoughts were creating a whole new reality!

As soon as he arrived in class, the science teacher began her lesson: "Today we're going to talk about the infinitely small and about how matter is created."

"Wow!" Jimi thought.

Here is the lesson, as heard through the ears of a child: "Blah… Blah… Blah… Until a few centuries ago, man believed that matter was made up of many tiny building blocks… Blah… Blah… Blah… But over the last hundred years or more... Blah… Blah… Blah… Scientists have discovered that when analyzed under a microscope, these blocks contain within them a very tiny world, which follows a different set of rules. This world is essentially *empty*. It's like a great blue sea, within which flow an infinite number of waves that can become *anything*." explained the teacher.

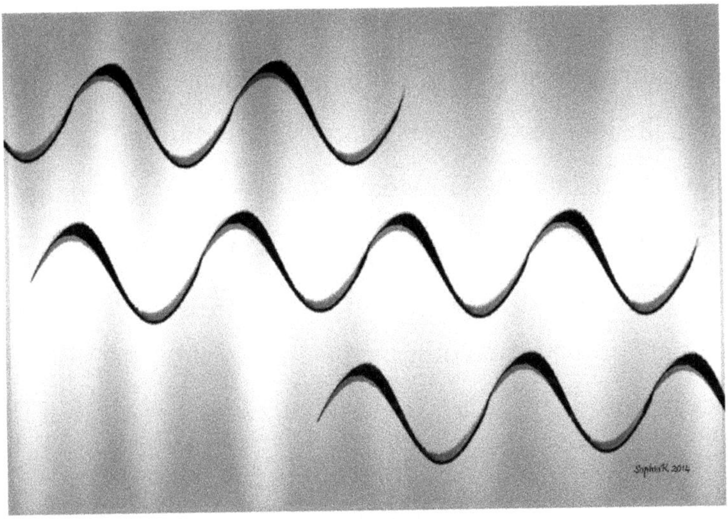

"*Like the Garden of Infinite Possibilities*!" Jimi thought.

"When someone observes one of these waves, it changes form and becomes a particle." the teacher continued.

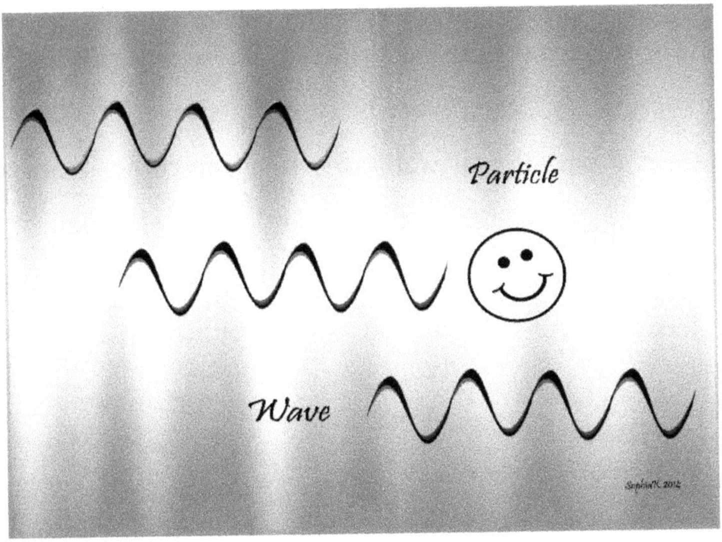

"Scientists say that the Observer creates reality." she added.

"*Thoughts become things!*" Jimi pondered.

In conclusion, the teacher said: "So, everything you see, take your desk for example, is made up from waves of energy which emerged from a sea of nothing to become particles, simply because someone had the idea to build this desk. These particles, rotating very quickly around each other, create the matter that you perceive as solid. Is this clear? Who would like to summarize what I've just explained?"

Jimi raised his hand and said: "*There are infinite possibilities*, in the form of waves, and they become particles when someone observes them. So, the imagination of the observer… can create anything!"

"Excellent, Jimi! That's exactly what science has discovered!" said the teacher.

"Now – she continued – I'd like to show you photographs of some experiments, which will help to better clarify this concept. These are two particles of water: the first one comes from a bottle labeled 'LOVE', the other one from a bottle labeled 'HATE'."

"Which one do you like best?" asked the teacher.

All the kids, now fascinated by the subject, said: "The one called love!"

Love

Hate

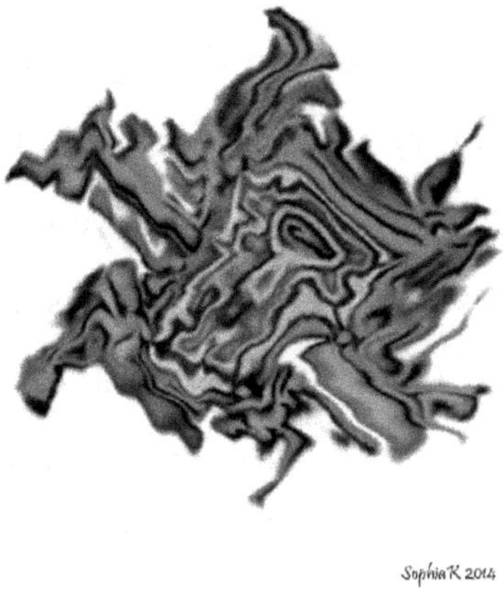

"Good! And who can tell me why this transformation occurred?" she asked.

"*Because thoughts become things*!" said Jimi.

"Congratulations! I can't think of a better way to explain it! You are a genius, Jimi!" complimented the teacher.

At this point, Jimi was overjoyed.

As soon as he walked out of class he jumped for joy, not only proud of the day's successes, but above all of the fact that he created them with his own thoughts.

Soon enough Jimi felt invincible and began to fantasize about all the things he could create.

It didn't take him very long to go from confident… to arrogant!

In the cafeteria line, Jimi cut in front of two younger kids who became very upset. He filled up his tray and headed straight for his favorite spot, near the window.

As he walked over to the table, however, he met John, a menacing, older boy who bumped against him on purpose, making all the food on Jimi's tray spill over, including his all-time favorite strawberry yogurt. Jimi didn't have the guts to say anything, but thought to himself: "What a bully!"

After a short game of basketball, he headed for the school bus. Along the way, a friend of his accidentally hit him with his schoolbag; Jimi got angry and yelled at him in front of everyone.

Once on the bus, though, he tripped and spilled some of his soda on the floor. The bus driver told him off and Jimi walked to the back of the bus thinking: "He sure is rude!"

Some of the magic from that morning had worn off after those small mishaps and Jimi started to become gloomier.

As soon as he got home and walked through the door, he found his mom in a terrible mood over a parking ticket she had just gotten. Rudely, she asked him to set the table and he thought to himself: "She sure is in a bad mood!"

After dinner, Jimi went to bed still confused by the highs and lows of his day, so with all of his heart he asked Blu to come back and answer more of his questions.

Outside, the wind was blowing strong and the moon shone over all the children curled up in their beds.

Jimi, content to be warm and cozy under the covers, fell asleep.

THE HOUSE OF MIRRORS AND THE BOOMERANG

CHAPTER FIVE

Shortly before midnight, Jimi heard an owl hooting loudly and opened his eyes.

Blu was there, sitting on the couch, smiling, with his radiant cloak made of pure energy.

"So, how was your day, Jimi?" asked Blu.

"The morning was perfect! You were right: by changing my thoughts I created many genius situations!" answered Jimi.

"But in the afternoon, I met a lot of obnoxious, rude and grumpy people."

"Ok, that's your personal view of events. Before experiencing another adventure, like the one you had last night, let's go over Rule n. 2 of the Garden of Infinite Possibilities." said Blu.

"*Thoughts become things.*" repeated Jimi.

"Good. You must always remember that *every reality*, even if unpleasant, *is created by you*!" said Blu.

"Now, let's look at the useful aspects of the encounters you described as negative. – continued the master – Have you ever been inside a House of Mirrors?"

"Yes, at the Amusement Park." answered Jimi.

No sooner had he finished his sentence, when mirrors appeared everywhere in his room.

"What do you see?" asked Blu.

"Me in my light blue pajamas."

"And now, if you were to dress like a soccer player, what would you see?" asked Blu.

"Me dressed like a soccer player." answered Jimi.

"And if you dressed up like a Halloween pumpkin?" asked Blu.

"Me dressed as a Halloween pumpkin" said Jimi giggling.

"What's your favorite outfit?" asked Blu.

"Jeans, red sneakers and a striped t-shirt."

"So if you wanted to see yourself in the mirror, dressed in that outfit, what would you have to do?" was Blu's next question.

"Well… I'd have to dress that way!"

"And that's exactly how life works, Jimi: life reflects our *mental… outfits*. When we're angry, we meet angry people and/or we experience violent situations; when we are loving, we meet loving people and/or we experience loving situations; and so on." explained Blu.

"Now that I think about it – reflected Jimi – I said that today I met some obnoxious, rude and grumpy people, but… actually I… was obnoxious to two little kids in the cafeteria; I also mistreated a friend who hit me with his schoolbag, which put me in a really bad mood. So… I mirrored myself in others?"

"Yes – answered Blu – and becoming aware of this, is very useful to quickly change one's attitudes. Isn't that fantastic?"

"Yeah. All I have to do is be aware and instead of blaming or judging others, change **MY** attitude!" exclaimed Jimi.

"Exactly! – said Blu – You will achieve great peace by knowing that everything is only a reflection of *you* and that… you can change anything, whenever you want to! Remember: *thoughts become things*."

At that point, the house of mirrors disappeared, but instead of returning to his bedroom, Jimi found himself in the middle of a beautiful desert. The earth had a reddish color, and rising all around were beautiful rocky mountains, which in their brown splendor, reflected the intense rays of the sun. It took just one look around, for Jimi to recognize what he'd only seen on TV documentaries: canyons, wild birds, cactuses and kangaroos.

"We're in Australia!" said the boy.

"Yes – responded Blu – We are here to talk about the *Boomerang Effect.*"

"You mean that curvy thing that, you throw and it comes back to you?" asked Jimi.

"Yes."

"Excuse me Blu, but what does that have to do with my attitude towards people?" asked Jimi.

"Think back – Blu said – to what happened today, after you cut in front of those kids in the cafeteria line."

"Umm… well John, this big kid who's a bully came along and pushed me, and made all the stuff on my tray spill over." Jimi admitted.

"And then, what happened after you yelled at your friend for accidentally hitting you with his schoolbag?" continued Blu.

"Umm… well, I accidentally spilled my soda on the bus and the driver yelled at me." said Jimi.

"So, what does that tell you?"

"That my actions come back to me?" asked Jimi.

"Exactly! And that, is the *Boomerang Effect*" confirmed Blu.

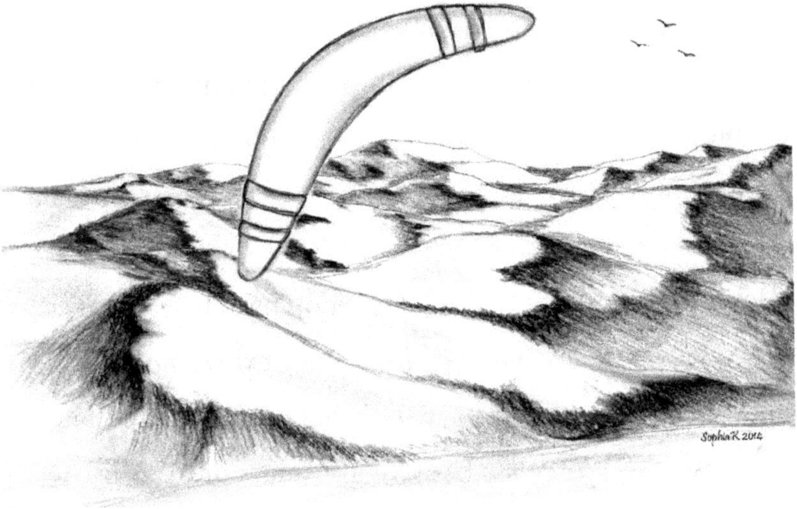

"Now that I think of it… my grandpa always used to say: "*You reap what you sow!*"" thought Jimi.

"That's right! That's just another way of expressing the same concept." Blu said.

"You see Jimi, this is a very important principle. Sooner or later we are destined to relive what we do to others. Actions that create good feelings, such as kind gestures or the act of helping, eventually come back to us in the form of equally pleasant emotions. The same goes for actions that create bad feelings, such as treating others cruelly. We end up experiencing the same form of treatment."

"As punishment, you mean?" asked Jimi.

"No – said Blu – In the Garden of Infinite Possibilities *there are no right or wrong actions*, therefore there are no prizes or punishments." he went on: "The feelings we caused in others, come back to us to help us understand the effects of our actions. It's a way of experiencing things through our attitudes. Oftentimes, that which we think we are creating with our actions, is very different than what we are in fact causing others to experience."

"Boy, I sure made lots of mistakes today!" said Jimi.

"Hey, take it easy Jimi! Try looking at it from another perspective: *there are no mistakes, only experiences*." said Blu. "Think about your sister Lili. How many times did she fall before she learned how to walk? How many times did she try to say a word before she actually pronounced it right?"

"Lots of times! But that's obvious. How else was she going to learn?" said Jimi.

"That's exactly right! – said Blu – Each one of us is constantly *evolving*. So, until we learn what it is we need to learn, we are destined to make attempts, and these attempts aren't mistakes, they are not wrong and they are not to be punished, they are just the steps of a ladder that lead to understanding: if we do not climb each one of them, we will never reach the top! Each experience, if we choose to learn from it, holds a lesson. Therefore, there are no mistakes or failures, only *lessons*."

"So… I shouldn't feel guilty?" asked Jimi.

"No. Guilt only makes you feel bad. If you need to apologize to someone, then do it. Learn from the experience and then move on." suggested Blu.

"Is that what wisdom is?"

"Yes, Jimi. *Wisdom* comes from experience, treasuring all emotions, good and bad, that come back to us, and learning the lessons. So – continued Blu – if something isn't going in the direction you desire, is it more constructive to feel as a failure, or… to feel wiser?"

"Wiser!" answered Jimi relieved.

"Excellent! You truly are… wise!" said Blu amused. "Now, I want you to think hard Jimi. I'm about to ask you a difficult question. What's the difference between telling ourselves that we are failures and telling ourselves that we are wiser?"

"Well… since thoughts become things… if I think I'm a failure, I'll keep experiencing failure, which means unpleasant situations; if I think I'm wiser, I'll create… more knowledge." concluded Jimi quickly.

"Congratulations! Perfect answer." said Blu. "Now, however, I want you to think about something else. Remember the photos you saw today at school about the water molecules? One exposed to the word 'love' and one exposed to the word 'hate'?"

"Yeah! The one exposed to the word 'hate' had an awful shape, it was deformed."

"Right. What is our body mainly made up of?" asked Blu.

"Water." said Jimi. And then he exclaimed: "I get it! When I think badly about myself, I'm harming my own cells and they even change form!"

"Very good! And that's the reason behind many diseases. You must always love yourself, my dear boy! No one else can do it for you!"

"Obviously – continued Blu – words can also hurt the cells… in other people! That's why I advise you, to always address everyone with kindness and love."

"Of course! – Jimi said – A lot of things make sense now!"

At that point, the sun became blinding. Jimi realized that what he was seeing in front of him wasn't a kangaroo but it was… his mom! She had opened the bedroom blinds to wake him up.

It was time to go to school!

The Mountain of Visions

Chapter Six

Jimi woke up in a great mood.

Treasuring his nighttime chats with Blu, he decided that he was going to be kind and tolerant with everyone he met that day.

Walking out of the house, he greeted everyone cordially, even people didn't know very well; when the school bus arrived he helped a girl get on and left the window seat for his friend Matt.

The mere fact that he did these acts of kindness, made him feel good and everyone gave him heartfelt thanks.

Near the school, Jimi noticed a woman who was giving some money to a person in need and he thought: "What a nice lady! She's helping someone she doesn't even know…"

Then he saw an elderly man working as a volunteer, helping mothers and children cross the street safely to get to school, and again he thought about how many things could be accomplished with love and kindness.

Jimi was realizing that the reality he saw around him stemmed from his own thoughts and attitudes: what he felt inside was manifesting outside as well.

That's when he remembered something Blu had said: "*As within, so without.*"

"It's not the outside world that creates our thoughts, but rather, it's our thoughts that create the outside world! – Jimi thought – Today I'm tuned into kindness and just like magic, I'm a part of acts of kindness, love and courtesy. This is great!"

With this new understanding, Jimi walked into class happy and cheerful.

The entire morning, he continued being kind to everyone and was very aware of his thoughts; therefore, everything went along beautifully.

However, when school was out, Jimi was faced with a new situation: some of his classmates were heatedly arguing over the soccer game they had played during recess.

"There you are! We were just waiting for you!" said Mike, one of the kids.

"Why me?" asked Jimi.

"Because it's your fault we lost the game!" accused Mike.

"That's not true! Why is it my fault?" Jimi said irritated.

"If you had passed the ball to Nick instead of Steve, he wouldn't have lost it to the other team and they wouldn't have scored a goal!" Mike growled.

"How do you know that? Maybe they would have stolen the ball from Steve as well!" continued Jimi.

"You guys don't get it! – another kid interrupted – Jimi should have just made the shot and not passed the ball at all! But he didn't do it because he's a coward!"

"I'm a coward? How dare you?" Jimi said.

"Hey, Jimi's right! – another boy stepped in – he didn't have a clear shot! But, he should've passed the ball back and not forward!"

"That's ridiculous! From that position, you don't pass it backwards... " said Mike.

This argument went on for a good fifteen minutes but was getting nowhere fast!

Jimi went from being happy and cheerful, to confused and disoriented because of this argument. He went home, did his homework and asked Blu to come back that night, to help him better understand.

That night Jimi's room was unusually cold. It felt like being outside on a winter night.

When Jimi got out of bed to get another blanket, his feet felt icy cold as they touched the floor and he thought to himself: "This carpet almost feels like snow!" Then he looked at the ground and said: "But… it is snow!" As he looked up, he found himself on the peak of a snowcapped mountain, with a beautiful blue sky overhead, dotted with pink fluffy clouds.

"Do you like this mountain?" asked Blu.

"Y… y… y… yes! Brrr, but it's freezing!" answered Jimi.

"Here, put on these ski clothes and you'll be nice and warm." said Blu.

"What a beautiful view! But… why are we here?"

"To answer the question you wanted to ask me this evening. I thought I'd get a head start!" smiled Blu.

"My question? – Jimi tried to remember – Oh! Yeah! I'd like to know why I felt so bad after that argument at school today. It upset me."

"Why did it upset you, Jimi?"

"Well… because I was right and everyone else was wrong!"

"I see – said Blu – By the way, do you know what this place is called? The Mountain of Visions."

"Cool!" exclaimed Jimi.

"Look – Blu pointed to the mountain slopes – there is a small village on every slope. Now let's call out to someone and ask them what they see."

Blu turned towards the village on the mountain's southern side and asked: "Excuse me madam! What do you see?"

"The sea!" answered the woman.

Then he turned to the village to the north and asked: "Excuse me, young man! What do you see?"

"The hills!" said the young man.

Then he turned to the village on the eastern side and asked: "Little boy! What do you see?"

"The desert!" said the little boy.

Lastly, he turned to the village on the western slope and asked: "Kind lady! What do you see?"

"The plains!" said the elderly woman.

"Who's right?" Blu asked Jimi.

"Well – said Jimi – They're *all* right… from *their* point of view."

"Exactly!" said Blu. "Wouldn't it be absurd if all these people started arguing over which view from the mountain is the right one; each one claiming that, it's just the sea, just the hills, just the desert, or just the plains?"

"Yes, it would be stupid." said Jimi.

"Well, think about how often people want to be right at all

costs, without considering that everyone sees things from their own *personal* point of view."

"I get it! – Jimi exclaimed – In the argument over today's game, everyone was right, because no one was certain which was the best move to have made!" Then he looked around and added: "We're lucky up here: from the peak we can see everyone's point of view!"

"You know why we see them all?" asked Blu.

"No…" said Jimi.

"Because we are willing to *respect* them all. Being on the peak doesn't mean being better than everyone else, it just means we understand that *there is no right or wrong*; there are *only different points of view.* This allows you to have your own opinions, to learn from other people's opinions and not to judge anyone."

"Wow! – Jimi said amazed – If everybody thought that way, there would be no wars, violence or fighting! Everyone would live in harmony!"

"You can choose to start thinking this way. – said Blu – We can only change ourselves; if in the darkness of ignorance we light our own small candle, maybe someone will follow our example and soon the darkness will become light!"

And in fact, everything had become clear to Jimi.

It was already morning, and time to go to school!

Where Clouds Are Born

Chapter Seven

As soon as he waked into the school's courtyard, Jimi's friends once again started up yesterday's conversation, and asked him to think about his moves, before playing the next game.

Jimi, empowered by last night's lesson said: "Guys, *you're all right, from your points of view*! Yesterday I followed my instinct and made that play. It seemed like the right move at the time. I'm sure today will go great!"

The other kids, who were expecting another argument to start up, answered: "Guess you're right Jimi, no one really knows what would have happened if you had made a different play. Come on, let's go play some hide and seek before class starts!"

Jimi realized how important it was to know how to deal with people, to respect everyone, without creating confrontations. With his tolerant answer, instead of an argument, he had created a spectacular play group!

His morning in school passed very quickly and Jimi, thanks to his nightly lessons with Blu and his daytime experiences, felt invincible.

This helped him get through a very difficult afternoon.

When Jimi opened the door to his house, his mother was holding Lili in her arms and crying.

Jimi's grandmother had died that morning.

In a flash, Jimi thought of all the love he had felt for that sweet, tender woman. She always had a loving caress for him, while she prepared her delicious apple pie or when she took some money from her purse for him to put in his piggy bank.

Jimi burst out crying and in the hours that followed he reminisced about all the wonderful moments he had spent with his grandmother, sometimes at the park, other times at home on a rainy afternoon, after school.

In Jimi's mind, all this had vanished forever – just like that - the moment he arrived home that day.

In the evening there was a service and for the last time Jimi saw his grandmother; looking infinitely sweet just as she always had. He cried a thousand tears and finally, exhausted, went to sleep.

Like he'd done all the other nights, Jimi asked Blu to come back, this time to help him understand how such a loving person was gone so suddenly.

After a few hours of sleep, the boy woke up and saw Blu standing in front of him.

Jimi burst out crying and his teacher lovingly held him in his arms, for a long while.

When he finally stopped crying, Jimi asked: “What happens when you die? Does it all just end? Where do people go?”

“Do you feel like going to the science lab?” suggested Blu.

“Yes. I like that place a lot.” said Jimi, and suddenly his room started filling up with bookcases overflowing with books, test tubes, microscopes, vials, work stations, skeletons and drawings.

“Here we are!” said Blu. “Now, Jimi, do you remember what the teacher said last time you were here in the lab?”

“Basically, the lesson was that… *nothing is created and nothing is destroyed.*”

“Can you explain what that means?”

“Well, I can give you an example.” Jimi said.

“If we take an *ice cube* and put it in the sun, it will melt and turn into water.”

“If we leave the *water* in the sun, it will evaporate and become a cloud.”

“Then when the *clouds* collide, rain will be created and thanks to the rain once again we will have *water*.”

“When the cold arrives, the water will again turn to *ice* and so on.”

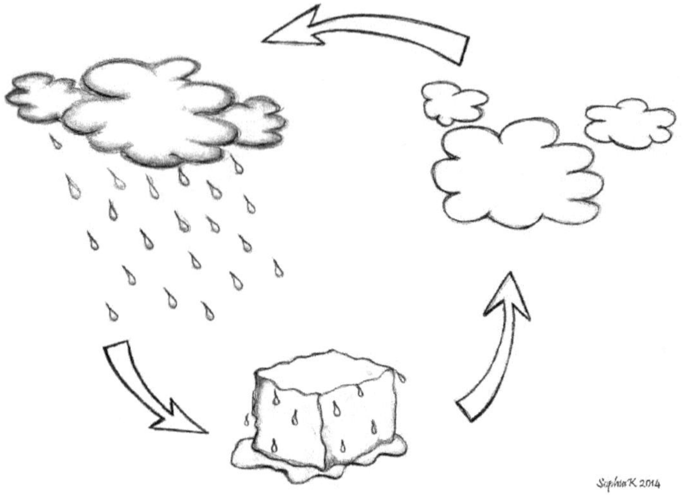

"Excellent example! – Blu said – So, Jimi, what's the moral of this story?"

"*That things change form, but never lose their essence.*"

"You amaze me, kid! I couldn't have said it better myself!" Blu congratulated Jimi. "Using a bit of imagination, let's apply this very principle to people as well. – continued Blu – When we live inside a body we have a certain form, just like the *ice*; when we leave our body, we are no longer visible to the naked eye, just like the *water* when it evaporates; then we go up to the sky, just like the *clouds*, and there we think about a place we'd like to rain on, so we can live another adventure. Once we have decided where, we become *rain* and when the time is right, we become *ice* again! We'll be a different ice cube, maybe in a different part of the world!"

"So there is no death! – exclaimed Jimi – There is only a change in form, in other words the body!"

"Like you said: *nothing is created, nothing is destroyed.* – reaffirmed Blu. – Don't you feel relieved knowing this?"

"Yes! Very! Because now I know that my grandma has left her body, but she's still alive and always will be! She'll just take on different forms!" said Jimi, thrilled.

"But now, I want to understand why people die, o better yet: why do they leave their bodies and how do they end up inside a new body?"

"Excellent questions, Jimi! – said Blu – Let's see if you like this visual: *life is a great adventure* in which there are infinite possibilities. Each one of us, deep down, is curious and wants to experiment as much as possible. For some adventures, though, the body we are in is not suitable. For example, could you see me as a ballerina, dancing around in a pink tutu?"

"Ha! Ha! Ha!" laughed Jimi hysterically! "With your build... how would you manage that? You'd look ridiculous! Ha! Ha! Ha!"

"I agree! I would look funny and most of all... I wouldn't be able to! I'm a big tall man, my body isn't made to dance gracefully like a delicate ballerina – said Blu – But let's suppose that I really wanted to have that experience. At the end of this life I would express my desire: I want to be a ballerina! And that desire, just like in the Garden of Infinite Possibilities, will create my new reality, with the right body and in the right environment."

"So – Jimi intuited – it's likely that most of the people I see have been, from one life to the next: men, women, poor, rich, violent, peaceful, beautiful, ugly, healthy, sick, policemen, thieves, and so on?"

"That's right. In order to experience different adventures." Blu said. "If you want, you can call it *reincarnation*."

"Sounds cool!" Jimi said.

"It's just an instrument." continued Blu. "It becomes cool, as you say, when you know how it works. Otherwise it has its downside."

"What's that?" asked the boy.

"Remember the Boomerang Effect?"

"Yes! *What I do to others comes back to me*; so I'll feel what they felt and I'll understand the impact of my actions." repeated Jimi.

"Exactly! And what would happen– asked Blu – if your actions didn't come back to you during the same lifetime, or if you didn't learn the lesson during your lifetime?"

"Maybe… they'd come back to me during another lifetime, until I learn the lesson."

"That's right, Jimi! So reincarnation is based both on new experiences you wish to have, and on old experiences from which you have yet to gain wisdom."

"So… – reflected Jimi – the wiser I become in this lifetime, the greater my freedom of choice is for the future?"

"That's exactly it! This is why I advise you to be kind to yourself and others and always be aware of the consequences caused by your actions!" suggested Blu.

"What if I have all the experiences that I desire, and understand the lesson of each one?" asked Jimi.

"*Then you would have no desire to reincarnate back here.*" said Blu. "Maybe you would choose another planet or another universe." the master continued.

"*Another planet*? *Another Universe*?" asked Jimi incredulous.

"Did you ever look at the stars at night, Jimi? How many are there?"

"They're infinite, I love looking at them!"

"Does it seem strange to you, that in the infinite sky… there would be other beings?" asked Blu.

"To tell you the truth, now that I think about it, it seems more than likely!"

"It's pure logic, Jimi, just pure logic." said Blu.

"But… if I wanted to… could I live in this body for hundreds of years or even… forever?"

"*There are infinite possibilities*, Jimi."

"But… I don't know anyone who's ever done that." confessed Jimi.

"That doesn't mean it is impossible." answered Blu.

"Right… – said Jimi – If you think about it, before the airplane was invented, it was thought impossible for man to fly!"

"Excellent example!" Blu enthusiastically exclaimed.

"One last question, Blu: what is *Heaven and Hell*?"

"You tell me! What do you mean by those two words?"

"Heaven is when you feel really good; and Hell is when you feel really bad." said Jimi.

"And do you need to die to experience these two states of mind?" asked Blu.

"Well, no… In the first case, I just need to have good thoughts and in the other bad thoughts. And the reality is created!"

"Perfect, Jimi! *Therefore, Heaven and Hell, are not physical places, they are just a state of mind.* The way we feel depends on our thoughts. No one forces us to think good or bad… It's our own choice!" said Blu.

"So… No, horns, flames and pitchforks?" asked Jimi.

"Absolutely not! – Blu laughed – Use those things to dress up for Halloween!"

The boy laughed as well!

The following morning, when he woke up in his bed, Jimi looked at the clouds wondering, what adventure his sweet grandmother planned on having next.

Before leaving for school, he thought to himself: "Grandma, I know you're alive even if I can't see you. But just to be sure, send me a sign, you know, like ghosts do! And have fun up there! Bye, grandma!"

The Island of Abundance

Chapter Eight

As soon as he arrived at school, Jimi ran into his teacher who looked at him sadly and said: "I'm so sorry, dear. I heard about your grandmother."

Jimi, without slowing his pace as he headed towards the playground, answered: "Don't worry, Miss: she's planning her next adventure!"

The teacher wasn't quite sure she understood what he said, but she was glad to see he was in good spirits!

It was a very pleasant day, even though the house was still filled with a sense of sadness after grandma's death. It didn't seem as though Jimi's mom and Mark were familiar with the ice-water-cloud-rain concept.

Furthermore, the two continued talking about how certain relatives had been insensitive, how some friends had disappeared during a time of need, about bills to be paid and other usual arguments.

Jimi was amazed by how unhappy most adults seemed to be and

decided to ask Blu why that is.

Once again that night, the master appeared, looking radiant as always.

Without hesitating, Jimi asked him: "If the rules of life, namely those of the Garden of Infinite Possibilities, are so simple, how come everyone isn't always happy and in full control of their life?"

"*Because, this isn't a free planet.*" answered Blu. "The rules of the Garden of Infinite Possibilities are not taught, they are kept hidden or ridiculed."

"How come?"

"Because that way, the few people that rule the world can control the majority of the population and make them work for their own personal interests."

"That's not possible! How can you control the entire world?" said little Jimi troubled.

"You tell me! – Blu answered – Do you like Nature?"

"Of course!"

Moments later, the most beautiful island Jimi had ever seen appeared before him: a huge, enchanted land emerged, with golden beaches, green mountains, waterfalls, forests, colorful birds and the most exquisite fruit he could ever imagine.

"Welcome to the Island of Abundance!" said Blu.

"Wow! It's amazing! The people who live here must be very happy!" said Jimi.

"Yes! It's a peaceful place where everyone can get everything they need from Nature. People here live in peace, they love and respect their island, they celebrate the seasons and the abundance of their harvest." said Blu.

"Now tell me, Jimi – continued the teacher – if you wanted to conquer this island and its people, steal all their resources and turn them into slaves, how would you do it?"

"I would never do that!" answered little Jimi shocked.

"I know you wouldn't! But for the sake of argument, let's just say you wanted to, how would you do it?"

"Well … first of all, I'd find a way to become their leader." said the boy.

"How?" asked Blu.

"I'd use my knowledge to make them think that it's more important to know history, culture and grammar, rather than simply enjoying Nature. I would somehow make them feel *inferior* and *as though they need help* in order to learn to live a better life."

"Sounds like a good plan! Go on."

"Once I obtained power because of my alleged superiority, I would educate them so that they *all shared the same way of thinking*. However, I would be very careful not to share any of my knowledge, except for the minimum necessary to keep them working hard; otherwise someone might become as good as me and regain their power."

"Smart move! Go on." Blu encouraged him.

"I would have to find a way to turn their work into something that would be beneficial for me. If they paid their taxes with fruit from nature, I would end up with tons of bananas I couldn't possibly eat by myself! So, I would have to invent something that I could collect and use as I wished. Like… *money*! – Jimi said – And I would do it in such a way, that I would be the only one who can print it up, and everyone would have to use it in order to be able to get anything! This way, they could only get money from me, and even pay me interest!"

"You're amazing! This is the plan of a true dictator! Any other ideas?"

"I'd have to do it in such a way, that no one would rebel! I'd have to invent some sort of *moral code*, a code of behavior. For example, I could say that I was the only God, or the only one qualified to talk on God's behalf, or maybe that I'm the only one who knows the true path to happiness. Whoever didn't obey the rules would… let's see… go to hell! This way, everyone would be scared and behave themselves." the boy finished with a satisfied look on his face.

"That's a classic! – Blu laughed – Ok, go on, Jimi."

"Well, I'd have to prevent people from discussing intelligent topics amongst themselves, otherwise they might figure out what's going on!" smiled Jimi mischievously. "I'd need *newspapers* that write only what I want them to and maybe even a *television network*, that way everyone would be distracted! Furthermore, since thoughts create things, if I get everyone to think like I want them to, that would create *my* reality and not theirs!"

"That's terrible!" congratulated Blu. "And what if you wanted to make even more money?"

"I could make up something to sell them. I could create the *need* to have, for example, pants or shirts, or a certain physical appearance, or new means of transportation or new homes. That way everyone would feel compelled to buy these things and they would work even harder in order to be able to afford them. And I would make lots of money both on sales … and on taxes!"

"That's genius, Jimi! – Blu said – And what if you wanted to stir things up once in a while? What would you do?"

"Well… I'd start a *war*. That way I could sell weapons and rebuild houses." concluded Jimi.

"Ok, Jimi. Do you see many differences between the plan you just devised and the way we actually live today?"

"Unfortunately… no!" answered Jimi sadly. "Now I understand what you meant when you said that we don't live on a free planet!"

"Good, I'm glad you gave all of this some thought." said Blu.

"But… – asked Jimi – can I still be free?"

"Of course! *Freedom is in your mind.*" answered Blu. "When you are fully aware of how the world works, you know how to *think for yourself*, therefore, you can *create the reality that* **YOU** *want*."

In the middle of the night, Jimi bolted upright from his sleep, sweating and thinking about how he had so easily forced an entire island of happy people into servitude.

"Certain subjects really get you thinking!" Jimi pondered to himself. "I want a better world so I'm going to start from me!" was the last thought he had before falling asleep again.

Shortly after… as he slept … he thought he heard Blu's voice saying: "I'm proud of you, kid!"

THE BIG FEAST

CHAPTER NINE

The following day Jimi decided to get up early and walk to school.

As he walked, he kept repeating out loud his new favorite sentence, which he had been using for some time, to create his day: "I have always been a genius!"

During class, he kept looking at Susie, the girl from the vending machine incident, and was convinced that he really liked her a lot. He decided to apply his new knowledge in order to create the opportunity for them to meet that afternoon.

He thought about the rules of the Garden of Infinite Possibilities: "*There are infinite possibilities*" and "*Thoughts become things*".

"It'll be a piece of cake!" thought Jimi.

After school, as he walked towards the park hoping to meet Susie, Jimi began to think about her, but was soon distracted by a shop window with skateboards.

After a while, he resumed walking and thinking about Susie, then he bumped into Matt and stopped to chat with him. As he started walking again, a *little voice* inside him was saying: "How can Susie like you? What are going to say if you meet her? Come on! She's never even said hello to you except for that one time!"

A bit distracted and discouraged, Jimi continued heading for the park.

Susie wasn't there, nor was she at the ballpark or anywhere along the way home.

Full of doubts and questions as to why he hadn't managed to create the opportunity for them to meet, once again that night Jimi asked Blu to come and help him understand. Assured that Blu would show up, he went to sleep early in order enjoy a night full of new adventures and understandings.

Around midnight, he felt someone shaking him awake.

"Hey, Jimi! First you ask me to come and then you won't wake up?"

"Oh! Hi Blu! Sorry... I was having a great dream! I was dreaming of a girl I know."

"Ok, so what's your question?" asked Blu.

"How come when you brought me to the *Garden of Infinite Possibilities,* everything happened right away but, in my everyday life I can't seem to quickly create encounters and situations that I want?" asked the boy.

"Do you like pasta, Jimi?"

"Sure, a lot! But what does food have to do with anything right now?"

In a flash, Jimi's room turned into the biggest and most professional kitchen the boy had ever seen: a large stovetop, copper pots and pans, shelves filled with all the ingredients you can think of.

"Will spaghetti do?" Blu asked.

"Yeah, perfect! – Jimi answered – But I'd like an answer, not a plate of pasta!"

"Relax Jimi, relax! Isn't it nice to enjoy life while learning?" Blu reassured him.

"Well… I guess so."

"Then, tell me in detail how to make a great spaghetti dish."

"First of all... we have to choose what kind of sauce we want. Let's say tomato sauce, for example. Then, we take a pot of water add some salt and put it on the stove. When the water has boiled, we throw in the spaghetti and after about 10 minutes we strain it. Then we mix in the sauce and we have a feast!"

"Exactly! The same applies to anything else we want to create." answered Blu. "The first step is to have *a clear idea* of what we want. The second step is to put our dream … '*on the fire*'."

"On the fire?" said Jimi, surprised.

"Yes. Our thoughts become things **IF** we focus on those thoughts." continued Blu. "'**FOCUS**' is the word the ancient Romans used for 'fire'. Today we use this term to mean: when our brain remains *concentrated on one thought for a long period of time*. Kind of like the burner under the pot of spaghetti: you can't turn it off before the pasta is cooked."

"Oh! I get it!" said Jimi happily "Otherwise, anything would materialize! For example: I think of a monster for a second, and a monster appears in my room!"

"Ok, if you want to put it that way." answered Blu. "If you really want something, the Garden of Infinite Possibilities knows it, because you keep thinking about it and so it creates it."

"Now let's talk about the water and the pot." said Blu. "The pasta takes 10 minutes to cook in a medium size pot with about 8 cups of water in it. What would happen, Jimi, if we were to make our two portions of pasta in a pot for 100 people with about 200 cups of water?"

"It would take hours!"

"That's right! Because we would be increasing the fire's *resistance*." explained Blu. "And what if we opened the window, allowing the wind to blow right on the stove, putting out the flame every so often?"

"We would end up eating tomorrow evening!" answered Jimi.

"You got it, kid!" said Blu. "Now, consider the thoughts you had about Susie today and tell me if you find any similarities with our pot of spaghetti."

"Let's see… – began Jimi – I had a clear idea that I wanted to meet Susie, so that part was right! Then, as a matter of fact, I thought about her on and off, without conviction, like I was turning the burner on and off again. I also let myself get distracted by a thousand other things, such as skateboards and friends, like opening the window and letting the wind blow on the stovetop. Plus, I didn't really believe that I would meet her: deep down I felt she didn't like me; it's like I chose a huge pot for a thousand people!"

"Bravo! You analyzed the situation perfectly!" answered Blu. "When you want something, you must have *a clear idea* of what it is you want, then *constantly imagine* it and *don't allow yourself to be distracted* by external things. *Remove any resistance*, like your doubts, and *firmly believe* that you will obtain it!" said Blu.

"Even *not believing* in what you want is a thought that will become a thing! And the result will be… that you won't obtain what you want!"

"I understand now!" said Jimi.

"Now, here's something else to think about…" Blu paused, and then asked: "Why do you want to meet Susie in particular?"

"Because I want to fall in love and she's really pretty." was Jimi's answer.

"And what if she has other plans?" asked Blu.

"I would be heart broken…" said Jimi sadly.

"So, Jimi, you're putting your life in someone else's hands?"

"You're right… I would have no control over the situation!" said the boy. Then he asked: "What's the wisest way to deal with this sort of situation?"

"Here we'll need help from my good friend Jean Pierre!"

Just as soon as Blu said his name, in came a tall man with a huge belly, round cheeks and a tall chef's hat.

"At your service, kind sirs!" bowed Jean Pierre.

"He's the best cook in the world!" said Blu introducing him.

"So, what would you like? Meat or fish?" asked Jean Pierre.

"I'd like meat!" said Blu. "I'd like fish!" said Jimi.

"Would you like a dessert as well?" offered Jean Pierre.

"Yes!" they both answered.

"Please be seated! I'll be with you in a jiffy!" said Jean Pierre.

Jimi and Blu sat across from one another, at a long fancy table, just like the ones you'd find in a castle used by kings and queens.

It was a candlelit dinner, in front of a majestic fireplace with a crackling fire.

A few minutes later, a series of waiters served an infinite number of courses, consisting of meat dishes for Blu and fish dishes for Jimi.

At that point, the child asked bewildered: "Why didn't Jean Pierre ask us exactly what dish we wanted?"

"Because he's the best cook in the world and this is the best restaurant in the world." answered Blu. "So, what you have been served, according to your preference, is the best there is, it's just that you don't know it yet!"

"Yum! In fact… everything is really delicious!" Jimi admitted.

"Would you have preferred spaghetti and hamburgers?"

"Definitely not! But I never would have chosen these dishes because I didn't know them."

"You see Jimi, life works in exactly the same way: it's an infinite banquet. Once you have expressed your preferences, you just have to *let yourself be surprised* by the many novelties and varieties that you may enjoy much more, than that which you are used to."

"So, for example, if I want to fall in love I should ask for **LOVE** and not Susie?" asked Jimi.

"Yes, Jimi! Many people suffer because they want a specific person, forgetting, that the other person also creates his or her own reality, which may not include them. It's exactly like you just did with the fish: you ask for the *category* you want, and rest assured that you'll get the best variety of tastes to choose from according to your preference! If there is one thing you don't like, you can always leave it and try something else. Maybe you'll fall in love with Susie, or perhaps Mary, Daisy or Lucy! If you're experiencing love with any one of them, it doesn't matter what their name is or what they look like: what counts is that *you're experiencing the emotion you wanted to have*!"

"What if I wanted *money*?"

"Same idea! – answered Blu – What do you want money for?"

"Because it gives me a sense of freedom. I could take my family to Disneyland!" was Jimi's first thought.

"Then ask for **FREEDOM**! – Blu continued – When you're free, by definition, you are free to do whatever you desire and therefore, will inevitably have the means by which to do it!"

"Of course! When I'm **FREE**, I'm **FREE** to travel, **FREE** to take some time off, **FREE** to have whatever I desire. Otherwise what kind of freedom would it be?"

"Exactly, Jimi! Remember the House of Mirrors? Life reflects back to you that which you are: if you love yourself and others, you'll have **love**; if you're free, you'll have all the means to enjoy your **freedom**." concluded Blu.

"Look, the desserts are coming! This is an excellent opportunity to give thanks for all this abundance!" exclaimed Jimi.

"Good thinking! You must always be grateful: life is a gift! Always treasure it!" said Blu.

"The best thanks – laughed Jean Pierre – is the fact that you have tasted everything!"

"Spoken like a true master!" commented Blu. "It is important to *make the most of all opportunities*!"

THE FOREST OF EVOLUTION

CHAPTER TEN

That morning Jimi was amazed that he wasn't hungry. Then he remembered all the wonderful things he had eaten with Blu the night before and laughed. To be honest… he even let out a little burp!

In school, during gym class, Jimi slipped and scraped his knee. Before he had a chance to get up, a girl named Jessie was standing in front of him, handing him a towel.

He had never noticed her before.

Perhaps she wasn't as pretty as Susie, but Jimi found her adorable. Her kindness opened his heart and he immediately saw a reflection of himself in her. He saw the same kind, independent, curious, luminous look that Jimi was beginning to recognize in himself.

"Thanks." said Jimi.

"No problem!" answered Jessie, and went back to playing.

Jimi looked for Jessie all afternoon.

When he finally found her at the park, near the river, they

played together the rest of the afternoon, happy to just be.

Susie was definitely out of the picture: now, for Jimi there was only Jessie!

The two of them saw each other every afternoon and you could even say that… they fell in love!

Jimi, filled with this new emotion, began to daydream about his future.

Unfortunately at the end of each day, he was confronted with his present, which did not allow him to fulfill his dreams.

So, one night, he asked Blu for inspiration again; as always, he appeared, looking radiant.

"What is your question tonight, Jimi?"

"In the past few days, I have made some big dreams: move to a new city, go live with my aunt and uncle and… become a great scientist."

"How wonderful!" said Blu.

"Sure, they're nice fantasies, but I think they're all impossible… Maybe my family won't let me go, and there just isn't enough money for me to enroll in a private school and university." Jimi said sadly.

Then he asked: "So, Blu, do I give up on my dreams?"

"A very good question! Follow me into the Forest of Evolution!" Blu invited.

From his cape an immense forest emerged; it was full of the grandest trees, all dressed in beautiful autumn colors, with crystal clear streams and vibrant green pastures, illuminated here and there with the sun's rays, which filtered through the branches.

That forest seemed very peaceful, but, after a closer look, there was actually quite a bit of traffic! Everywhere he turned, Jimi saw large and small animals hard at work: squirrels in search of nuts, ants carrying food, ladybugs flying everywhere, bees feasting on a thousand colorful flowers and many butterflies with the most magnificent wings.

"What beautiful butterflies!" said Jimi.

"Why do you like butterflies?" asked Blu.

"They radiate a sense of freedom and lightness…" answered the boy.

"Do you know the story about the Sea Butterfly, the one with the blue and gold wings that you see up there?" asked Blu.

"No, I didn't even know there were Sea… Butterflies! Tell me the story!"

So Blu began his story: "The Sea Butterfly is the bravest of all butterflies! It was born many, many centuries ago, right here in this very forest, where a caterpillar named Audacious used to live.

Audacious spent his days on this tree. He ate little green leaves, chatted with all the insects you see around here, and was always very careful not to end up in the web of a spider or be the target of some little bird.

His days were all the same and he just kept getting fatter.

Audacious was happy because he had everything he needed to

survive, the forest was always very abundant, but he was unhappy because he didn't have what he needed to *experience*: ***adventure***.

Every once in a while he would climb to the top of the tree and catch glimpses of all the wonderful far away places that he, with his build, would never be able to reach.

Given his little, chubby body, Audacious just didn't see how it could be possible. For many months he thought about giving up looking at his beautiful landscapes; actually, he almost decided that he would never again climb to the top of the tree to see them, so as not to feel so hopeless.

One night, he crept inside the trunk of this magnificent tree and had an amazing dream: he dreamt he was a colorful, graceful butterfly; he dreamt of flying from flower to flower, across the valleys he had seen from the treetop. Scents, breezes, and colors swept through Audacious's little body, and he felt like never before.

That dream was so captivating that he didn't wake up for a long time. Every now and again, he would regain consciousness and feel as though he were melting. He was losing interest in the little world he had been living in, for all those little green leaves he was used to eating and the boring chitchat with the other insects. He didn't know who he was anymore and he could see his body liquefying.

That dream was intoxicating!

And so, Audacious continued to dream ...

Then one morning, he looked at himself and... he wasn't himself anymore!

He was dressed in wings of blue, that were trimmed with gold; he had long legs and a thin, flexible body!

When he tried to move, Audacious was gently swept into the air by a breeze and he soon found himself flying over the treetops, seeing the blue sky with no obstacles to get in his way!"

"Did he get to the valley?" asked Jimi.

"Yes. – said Blu – And he enjoyed every minute of his journey! Curious, he explored everything and tried out all of his new talents."

"And why is he called a Sea Butterfly?"

"Because when Audacious arrived in the valley, he saw another beautiful landscape in the distance, something he hadn't been able to see even from the highest treetop in the Forest of Evolution. He couldn't imagine that beyond the valley, so far away, existed so much shimmering water, the color of azure by day, when kissed by the rays of the Sun, and a midnight blue by night, caressed by the moon who loved to gaze upon her reflection on its surface."

"And then what?" said Jimi impatiently.

"For many days, Audacious crossed many valleys, streams and hills, until he finally reached the much desired beach, where he could finally experience a new world."

"Did he stay there?"

"No – continued Blu – because Audacious, at that point, saw a huge sailboat in the distance and wondered where it was going. So, he flew all the way to the sailboat and perched on its bow, smelling the salty air. Soon after, the ship set sail and Audacious thought: "This is a true *adventure*!"

During the voyage, the little butterfly saw many wondrous and unimaginable things: great storms and endless horizons, multi-colored birds and jumping fish. Until one day, during a beautiful sunrise, when the ship arrived in an enchanted land. He didn't recognize any of the things he saw: the water was crystal clear, the trees bore the sweetest fruit he had ever seen and the flowers were of extravagant colors the shape of goblets filled with intoxicating perfumes. Audacious had arrived at the Tropics." said Blu.

"And then what happened?" asked Jimi.

"After a long time in that enchanted land, our brave little butterfly embarked on another sailboat and after a thousand adventures returned to the Forest of Evolution, where he told everyone about all the things he had seen. But no one believed him! Such wondrous things *were beyond the limits of their imaginations*.

One day, though, a little caterpillar, who was also a dreamer, was so captivated by the stories Audacious told that he decided to experience that adventurous voyage as well. And thus began the lineage of the Sea Butterflies." concluded Blu.

"How beautiful! I think I've learnt lots of things from this story." said Jimi.

"Good! Like what?"

"First of all – said the boy– I shouldn't be afraid to dream big."

"Yes, Jimi! *Dream what you desire, not what you think is possible*!" encouraged Blu.

"Then – continued the boy – I shouldn't let my present circumstances discourage me."

"Great! – said Blu – *Don't judge by appearances*! A caterpillar is just… a butterfly, that no one can see yet!"

"Then – Jimi added – just like Audacious did during his transformation, I must be open to change!"

"Exactly! – said Blu – If you *want* more, you have to *be* more."

"Furthermore – continued Jimi – I must overcome my fears and leave behind the world I know and am used to: I can't be both a caterpillar and a butterfly!" said Jimi.

"That's right! – said Blu – *What the caterpillar sees as* "the end of the world*", the butterfly sees as* "the beginning*"*!"

"Then – said Jimi – I must be daring and willing to experience a new reality!"

"I agree! –Blu said – *It's better to be an amateur butterfly than an expert caterpillar!*"

"And finally – said Jimi – every time I achieve a dream, it serves as the springboard for bigger dreams!"

"Excellent! – concluded Blu – *Never judge the future with the eyes of the present!* Even though right now you can't see all the pathways, life has the infinite in store for you, if… you're willing to take it!"

Jimi was very happy: he had finally understood the importance of holding on to his dreams!

During the night, he dreamt of butterflies everywhere, of course!

When he woke up, he looked out the window and for the first time, noticed a tiny crawling caterpillar, which made him reflect on the infinite potentials that even the tiniest creature can possess.

Then, remembering the story of Audacious, he thought: "If a caterpillar can become a butterfly, a human being can definitely change schools and move to a new city!"

He ran towards the school bus, still wrapped up in his dream.

An Extraordinary Revelation

Chapter Eleven

In the afternoon, all the kids went to the park, to watch a skateboard competition.

The biggest local champions were on the ramps.

Jimi had also brought his skateboard.

Overly excited by all their amazing stunts, on his way home, Jimi was going a little faster than usual and as he attempted to jump over a pothole, he fell and hurt his leg.

At the hospital the doctors stitched Jimi up telling him he had to stay home, possibly in bed, for at least three days.

His mom came to pick him up, scolding him all the way home and up until she got him to his room.

Jimi couldn't believe it: three days in bed! He couldn't see his friends, he couldn't see Jessie, and he couldn't go to his garden. Major boredom was in the forecast!

The next day, not knowing what else to do, Jimi began reading a book his grandfather had given him a few months earlier, called

The Genius Story. It was a narrative about great scientists and thinkers who had left their mark on human history.

After a few pages, Jimi was impressed by a thought concept expressed by one of the characters: "*Within every problem an opportunity can be found.*"

"Ok! – Jimi thought – I'll transform this accident into an opportunity to learn! Who knows... it may turn out to be useful some day."

Another thought stated in the book also fascinated the little reader: "All information is already available. One just has to ask a question and wait for the answer: it's called 'inspiration'. *A genius doesn't think, he is inspired.*"

The example from the book cited Isaac Newton who, after spending days and nights in his laboratory studying, discovered the Law of Universal Gravitation... sitting under a tree, when an apple fell on his head!

"*Await for the inspiration*. Interesting!" Jimi thought.

Reading on, the boy realized that virtually all great thinkers had to confront ***spirituality*** and did so, with some important questions: Is there a God? And if so, who or what is it? What's his role?

These were the same questions that Jimi had for a long time! So, once again that night, he asked Blu to come back and address this topic.

As always, a dazzling blue light lit up his room.

"Hey there kid! You have big questions tonight, huh?" smiled

Blu.

"Yep! – Jimi exclaimed – It seems to me, regarding God, we all have very different ideas, so as not to say... confused!"

"Of course! But let's be clear here, Jimi: in this case as well, I can only speak *my* truth. So my answers will only be a *fairytale,* until you apply your own reasoning into experience, in order to find your own truth. Agreed?" said Blu.

"Yes, it's a deal! But now, can you answer some of my questions?"

"Sure, Jimi! But first, before we begin, I want to know your point of view on the subject: do you believe in God?"

"I don't know... – answered the child – when I look into people's eyes, like my sister Lili or my girlfriend Jessie, I sense that there's something magical in them, and the same thing happens when I observe Nature, flowers or animals. It's almost as though everything is held together by some kind of poetry: I'd call it ***love***. But I don't like the idea of an old man with a beard looking down at us from the sky, judging whether we're good or bad. I also, don't find the story of Adam and Eve very convincing: all that fuss over an apple?"

"I see." Blu paused for a moment. "So it seems to me that you believe in a God, but you don't like the way he's been portrayed to you."

"Exactly! – Jimi said – No story I've heard has ever fully convinced me. And I don't like believing in things I don't understand!"

"Well, it's time to go back to the *Garden of Infinite Possibilities.*" In the blink of an eye, the two found themselves back in the garden, under a beautiful, bright blue sky.

"So Jimi, since you believe in God but you don't know what he is, if you had to somehow identify him in this place, how would you do that?"

"With the garden itself!"

"Why?" asked Blu.

"Because it's the origin of all things." answered Jimi.

"I agree!" said Blu. "The Garden, or God if you prefer, is the *father* and *mother* of all things."

“Mother?” Jimi said astounded. “But… Isn’t God male?”

“To make a child is a father enough or do you also need a mother?” asked Blu.

“Well, you also need a mother.” added Jimi.

“Then why does it surprise you to hear that God is also the mother?” smiled Blu.

“As a matter of fact, now that you got me thinking about it, it does make sense.” answered the boy.

“Now tell me, Jimi, who commands what the garden must create?”

“I do. My thoughts become things.” he answered.

“So now think: if the garden is God, who is the only one who can give God orders?”

“God himself!” answered Jimi and remained silent for a moment.

Then, amazed, he continued: “Wait, are you trying to say… that… **I AM** God?”

“Yes, Jimi *and so are all other people.* It is plain logic.” said Blu.

“In fact – thought Jimi – God wouldn’t take orders from anyone, other than himself!”

Then he said, astonished: “***I am God***: no one had ever told me that!”

“Do you know why no one ever told you that?” asked Blu.

“Because otherwise I would have become *free*? – said Jimi –

Just what I wanted to prevent the inhabitants of the Island of Abundance from becoming?"

"Exactly! –Blu answered – When you know that *there are infinite possibilities* and that *your thoughts become things*, you can create YOUR OWN reality and *no one can enslave or manipulate you*!"

"Now I understand lots of things!" said Jimi enthusiastically. "But what does Science have to say about this?"

"You tell me." said the master. "According to what you learned in science class, do you see a big difference between the phrases: "*There are infinite possibilities*" and "God is almighty" or "The ways of the Lord are infinite"?"

"No." answered Jimi.

"Do you see a big difference between the phrases: "*Thoughts become things*" and "Ask and you shall receive"?"

"No… the meaning is the same …" Jimi said.

"We live in wonderful times – said Blu – in which science has been able to prove in the laboratory what certain spiritual masters have been teaching since ancient times. Now it's easier to really understand how things work!"

"Wow! Everything is much clearer now." Jimi confessed. "But… I have other questions …"

"Shoot!" encouraged Blu.

"What is God's plan for me?" asked Jimi.

"*God doesn't have a plan for you.*" Blu answered. "*You are the one who must have a plan for God!*"

"Me?!?"

"Think about it, Jimi: when you enter the Garden of Infinite Possibilities, does someone suggest what you should create? Does someone dictate what you should create? Does someone dream for you?" said Blu.

"Well, no! I'm the one who decides what I want to do in the Garden of Infinite Possibilities."

"And what if you thought of nothing?" asked Blu.

"Then nothing would grow."

"So, what does that tell you?"

"That God, or the Garden of Infinite Possibilities, is created according to my imagination."

"Exactly! – Blu said – To put it more poetically, YOU *are the dreaming part of God.*"

"And why does he need me?" asked Jimi, feeling very small.

"Because Infinite Possibilities are just... *possibilities*, until someone gives them form through their dreams." answered Blu. "The Garden is very curious! *Thanks to your dreams, life expands*. Through you, God experiences its Infinite Possibilities. Your function is to ***create new experiences***: *to explore the unfamiliar.*"

"So – continued Jimi – *there's no need for a mediator between me and God?* Someone to tell me what to do?"

Blu provocatively turned the question around: "To speak to your mother or your father, do you need to go through your cousins?"

"No!" answered Jimi.

"Well then, there you go!" concluded Blu.

"You're right… – said Jimi – the Garden allows me the *freedom* to do or not do anything I want. My every thought is created without any filters or judgment!"

"Exactly! – answered Blu – This is called ***Free Will.***"

"Cool! I've never thought of myself as… a dreamer on behalf of God!" smiled Jimi.

"Never stop dreaming, my friend! And enjoy the marvels of your uniqueness, as it emerges and leaves you in awe."

"Wow!" thought Jimi, still elated by all the freedom he felt coursing through his body.

"Isn't it fantastic? – Blu exclaimed– Now that you've learned this new lesson, I want to celebrate! Come on Jimi, let's go to a special place!"

Shortly, the two were near the forest, on a hill overlooking the city.

"What's so special about this place, Blu? This is the city hillside!"

"Describe what you see." he answered.

"A beautiful starry sky, the river glistening under the moon, the forest with all its nocturnal animals, the autumn leaves rustling in the wind and much more..."

"And doesn't this view seem special to you?" asked Blu.

"Yes! Actually… I often take for granted some of the wonders of the day."

"And nighttime wonders too!" laughed Blu.

The teacher grew a bit more serious and remained silent for some time.

He observed the horizon, admired the sky, took in the scents of the forest and then, turning slowly towards Jimi, looked him straight in the eye and said: "My teachings are finished."

"No! Please Blu, don't go!" begged Jimi.

"Now it's time for you to put into practice everything you've learned." he answered. "My words will be of no use, until they become *your* own experience."

"I understand. – said the little boy, sadly – But... how will I get by without a master teacher?"

"You will meet other teachers along your path. – Blu answered – But always remember Jimi, *your only true master will always be...* YOU!"

"And when I don't know which path to take, how will I decide?" asked the child.

"*Always follow what you love*, even when it seems unattainable, and *listen to the voice of your soul."* said Blu. "This will keep you on the right path. When you come across a difficult situation along the way, remember that it is there to teach you the *lesson* you need. Always treasure these lessons!"

Then the teacher, with a big and loving smile, encouraged the boy: "Whenever you're going through a hard time, always remember… *the sun is always shining, clouds just come and go*!"

"Now I must leave …" concluded Blu.

"Wait! – Jimi held him back one more minute – I have one last question: who are you … really?"

"My name is *Jimi*." answered Blu.

"Just like me!" said Jimi happily.

"Yes, because I… am you!" said Blu uncovering his face.

"I am you in the future. I am your evolution. And I've come to take care of you during this difficult time in your life. I love you, my boy. I'm proud of all your progress! Keep it up! One day we'll be reunited and we'll spend the rest of our lives together!"

Seconds later, Blu and his beautiful cape vanished into thin air, leaving Jimi dumbfounded.

Surprise!

Chapter Twelve

The next morning, Jimi woke up feeling energized. He went to the bathroom to brush his teeth and with all the enthusiasm and warmth that only a child could have, looked at himself in the mirror and said: "Hi God! You're looking great today!"

A few weeks passed and Jimi had time to rethink about all the extraordinary revelations he had learned during those adventurous nights.

His days were now definitely better compared to those dark days of the past, in which he had laid in his bed crying and desperate, begging for answers.

Now, Jimi had his newly acquired knowledge and a good deal of experience under his belt.

His thoughts were fixed on his dream of moving to a new city and becoming a scientist. Although he intensely envision this every day, Jimi didn't see any concrete results for months.

Nonetheless, he wouldn't give up, always remembering that "*pasta needs to stay on the fire until it's cooked!*"

One afternoon no different from many others, as he walked carefree through the city streets, he saw an ad pinned to a bulletin board: "*School for Child Geniuses – entrance exams tomorrow at 4:00pm, at the Public Library.*"

Jimi thought: "Well... Since I've always been a genius... I'll definitely get in!"

The next morning, he woke up very determined and decided to put his knowledge to good use in order to be admitted; so, before leaving home, he mentally reviewed all that he had learned with Blu.

That afternoon, he went to the entrance exams where he started to feel a bit anxious, unsure as to what kind of test he was going to have to take.

A few minutes later, one of the examiners, Mr. Smith, walked in and said: “Welcome! Don’t worry everybody: today there won’t be any difficult exercises or tests.”

All the kids cheered happily!

“Settle down, settle down! – Mr. Smith went on – As I was saying, today you’ll be assigned an essay in which you will be asked to express your thoughts freely. In fact, at the School for Child Geniuses we’re not interested in your technical knowledge, but rather, in your open mindedness, therefore in your ability to learn and create extraordinary things. So… here is the theme of the essay: “*Is the glass half full or half empty?*” You have thirty minutes. Good luck!” concluded Mr. Smith, sitting down behind his desk.

The kids looked around confused, and soon, began to split into diverse groups.

“The glass is half empty!” said some kids.

“No, it’s half full!” said others, and a great murmur arose.

“This is a personal essay! – the examiner said loudly – Please work silently on your own! Thank you.”

Then the kids all bowed their little heads and began writing, each one supporting their own view point.

Jimi didn’t know how to answer the question.

He remained still for a while, looking at the other kids, some of which had already written two or three pages.

After twenty minutes, Jimi began to worry: he still hadn't written a word and time was almost up!

Suddenly, he remembered the book he had read when he had injured his leg, and the one sentence in particular which had really impressed him: "*A genius doesn't think. He asks a question and waits for inspiration.*"

So that's what Jimi did: he silently asked the essay question and waited for inspiration.

Minutes later, his hand furiously began to write.

This was Jimi's essay:

"*Title:* Is the glass half full or half empty?

Response:

The glass is *both* half full *and* half empty: it's the Observer who determines reality.

Since thoughts become things:

– he who sees the glass as half full, will create a life which is half-full;

– he who sees the glass as half empty, will create a life which is half-empty.

Both observations are correct and I respect them equally.

I, on the other hand, desire to create a *full reality* and I'm interested in life's infinite possibilities.

Therefore, in my observation, I see the glass as completely full: where there is no water, there is air.

Life doesn't present us with shortcomings: only

opportunities!"

Jimi handed in his essay and went to the lobby to wait for the results.

The essays were collected and brought into the conference room.

That was a special day because Mr. Smith was not the only one reviewing the essays; there was also the legendary scientist who had invented the time machine in a top-secret government project: Professor John Alchemist.

He was a man of few words, eminent and respected by all. He toured the country in search of a special child, one who would be able to grasp extraordinary concepts for futuristic projects, yet to be invented.

Mr. Smith brought the essays to the scientist who began reading them.

He quickly discarded most of them commenting: "These kids are all in search for the right answer. Half full or half empty. They are still on the path of collective thinking."

Prof. Alchemist was about to lose heart and give up, when he saw the last paper; Jimi's essay, was just a few lines written on one page, simple and effective.

He carefully read it over three times.

Tears welled up in his eyes. The man of Science was deeply moved.

In that essay he recognized his own childhood intelligence; he saw the potential of the same dreams that had inspired his studies.

"I found him!" exclaimed Alchemist.

A few minutes later, Jimi met the famous scientist in the conference room.

"Congratulations, young man! – said Alchemist – You have been accepted! Welcome aboard!"

"Thank you Professor, but… I think you should know that I'm not really very good in school, I wouldn't want to disappoint you." said Jimi.

"I don't care where you come from – Professor Alchemist reassured him – I only care about… where you want to go!"

"I want to *create new things* and *explore infinity*!" Jimi said, with a childish enthusiasm.

"Music to my ears! – said the Professor satisfied - I'll see you at this address in two weeks." and he handed Jimi his business card.

"Hey… this is the city where my aunt and uncle live!" thought Jimi, full of joy, seeing his dream becoming a reality.

"Professor – said the boy – you should know that my family doesn't have much money… I don't know how I will be able to move!"

"It will all be paid for, dear boy! You will be part of a research project for genius children. Now go home and tell your parents to contact me. Goodbye."

Jimi was walking on air. In his imagination he was no longer on Earth! He was in a futuristic place.

As soon as he got home, little Jimi enthusiastically recounted the whole story.

His mom couldn't believe it: her son was a genius!

Mark walked over to Jimi and said: "I always said you were a smart kid!" Jimi, on the other hand, remembered all the times in which Mark had treated him like he was less than zero. However, staying faithful to his recent evolution, he answered like a true master, forgetting the past and looking towards the future: "Thanks Mark! Thanks for the vote of confidence."

After some celebrating and the official acceptance confirmation to the new school, the boy went to get some well deserved rest.

He took his laptop, crawled under the covers and began writing a list of all the important things he needed to bring with him. But, being so tired he soon fell asleep with the computer still on.

The following morning, Jimi woke up to find his on his computer screen, an entire page with the word: "JIMI – JI" written all over it.

Confused and surprised, the child thought: "But… what's going on? Who wrote this? It's impossible! Besides… no one knows the nickname JIMI – JI! Only Grandma used to call me that. It was our secret!"

Then, stunned, Jimi remembered.

He began crying for joy: "Grandma! Grandma! – Jimi said– This is the sign I asked you for! Then it's all true! You are planning another adventure!"

And that truly was the best news of all.

After a while, Jimi looked out the window and while admiring the view, he remembered another phrase from that book about great scientists and thinkers: “The organ of sight is not the eye; it is the brain. *You only see what you believe*. Therefore, you must not see to believe, but rather… *believe to see*!”

He looked outside carefully, and reasoning upon that which he had recently learned, he went *beyond appearances*.

At first, he automatically saw the sky, the hills, the river, the trees, the flowers, the houses;

then he saw objects such as fruit from the Garden of Infinite Possibilities;

then he saw them as atoms and electrons;

then as pure energy;

then as God;

then – consequently – as… ***himself***.

It was a very brief but intense moment.

Jimi, suddenly understood that he had found the combination to unlock the vault in which he had been living for so many years, a prison of the mind, feeling alone and separated from life.

Thanks to that illumination, to that small, simple reasoning that reconnected him to Infinity, Jimi let go of all the worries, insecurities, and fears that had plagued him in the past.

He realized that, at only ten years of age, he was already the master of his life.

Then, feeling as though he had become a magician, treasuring all that he had learned, he uttered the phrase that made up the last number of the vault's combination:

"I can do anything! **I AM** infinite possibilities! The only limit… is my imagination!"

And so that day, the vault door swung open… revealing the greatest treasure there ever was: *Jimi's life*.

ACKNOWLEDGEMENTS

First of all, I wish to thank **all the people that have crossed my path in life.** Each one of them, in their unique way, even if just for a brief or apparently insignificant encounter, has served as a *master* teacher who added to the building blocks of my comprehension of things.

Thanks, in particular, to all those who brilliantly participated in this project: **Sophia Kountzeri**, **Federica Piacentini**, **Marina Petruzzi**, **Manuela Fuliotto, Francesco Manzitti, Alessandro Fellegara, Gianluca Pistore, Giovanna Carotti, Daniela Piccolo,** and **DJ Claudio Coccoluto** (whose music made me dream as I was writing this story).

My thanks also go to all the people who have played a fundamental role in my life: **my parents** who, upon discovering they were going to have me at a very young age, decided to bet on me, to "keep me" and to give me life; **my grandparents**, for inspiring me with their wisdom and tenderness; **my children Alice and Giorgio** whose questions prompted me to look for answers; my ex-wife **Francesca Felletti**, for introducing me to love at a young age, for helping me to evolve and grow as a man and for giving me two wonderful children; my primary school teacher, **Gianni Casarino**, for making me read, at only eight years of age, "*Jonathan Livingston Seagull*" (R.Bach) and "*Animal Farm*" (G.Orwell), leaving an indelible mark in my vision of the world;

Giorgio "Bongo" Contati and **Marco Contati**, for introducing me to the world of competitive *skateboard* and to the world of 1980s' *hip-hop*; **Dj Francesco Farfa** for his *avant-garde* electronic sound who opened me to new worlds and to freedom of thought; **Dj Roby J** for his music, his integrity and authentic friendship; **Elisabetta Ancona**, for introducing me to *Reiki*; **Vito Carlo Moccia** for providing inspiration and for treating me with integrity and mastery; **Stefano Fracassi**, my best friend, for making me a better person and for being there when I need him, making me truly comprehend the saying: *"A friend is worth his weight in gold!"*; **Roberto Re**, for his book "*Leader of Yourself*" and his courses which offered me the chance to meet people who became key figures in my future; **Alfio Bardolla**, for his teachings and for giving me wonderful opportunities, both in personal growth and in business; **Simone** and **Stefania Sorbara Galvez**, for introducing me to the exciting world of *network marketing*; **all of the wonderful persons in my network marketing's downline,** for getting in the game, in an adventure out of the ordinary, with courage and without any prejudice, understanding that a great oak… started with a small seed; **Carlos** and **Maria Calçada Bastos** for initiating me to the idea of "*Wonderland*", to the concept of non-identity and to some of the key concepts in this book.

Thanks to the magical village of **Spinello (Italy)** and to its people, for welcoming me amongst its wonderful mountains, for teaching me the harmony found in nature and the people who live in it, and thanks to its amazing and breath-taking views, which inspired some scenarios of this book, including the Garden of Infinite Possibilities.

Thanks to **Ramtha's School of Enlightenment** – the teachers, staff and students – for making, on a daily basis possible… the impossible!

Thanks to **JZ Knight**, whose extraordinary life filled with love, research, evolution and service has been an inspiration for the entire world.

Last but not least, a thank you – which words cannot fully express, because it transcends them – goes to my beloved Master Teacher, for whom I have infinite love and endless gratitude, **Ramtha** the Enlightened One, Lord of the Wind, whose teachings have greatly inspired this book.

CHARITY

I'm very grateful to Life for giving me the opportunity of being alive and for providing me with infinite possibilities to create and experience, always supported by universal Love.

This book was not conceived by me, it was inspired; it simply came through me by a stream of consciousness.

So I have decided to give thanks for the creative opportunity I received by giving back to charity **20%** of all profits made from this book, after taxes.

As beneficiary of the proceeds, I have currently chosen the ***Phoenix Rising School*** in Yelm, WA. U.S.A. (*thephoenixrisingschool.org*). It is a School that fosters the infinite possibilities of children, who are seeds of the future.

It is also my wish, should I have the honor of being called, to host book presentations and readings, to use these opportunities to **raise more funds for charity**.

Any initiative to this end is welcome, so please feel free to send any proposals, in both Italian or English, via *email* to the following address:

info@thegardenofinfinitepossibilities.com

CPSIA information can be obtained
at www.ICGtesting.com
Printed in the USA
FSHW011322230419